Read all About It
(Daft amusing and downright bizarre newspaper headlines)
by
Nick Weatherhogg
ISBN: 978-1-9999129-7-0

Published by

i2i Publishing. Manchester.
www.i2ipublishing.co.uk

CHAPTERS

1. Did They Mean That?

Springfield police charged one-armed man with unarmed robbery

MassLive.com

Friday 11th May 2007
One-armed man applauds the kindness
of strangers

Tulsa World

Tuesday 16th December 2003
Midget sues grocer cites belittling
remarks

Chicago Sun-Times

Sunday 17th October 2010
N.J. Judge to rule on nude beach

The Occasional Fish

Friday 24th October 1975
Juvenile court to try shooting
defendant

Deseret News

Saturday 9th August 1975
Astronaut takes blame for gas leak
Kentucky New Era

Monday 6th October 2003
Kids make nutritious snacks
Newsnight Newsletter

Wednesday 26th June 1996
Poverty meeting attracts poor turnout
Gooding County Leader

Monday 20th May 2013
Big rig carrying fruit crashes on 210
Freeway creates jam
Los Angeles Times

Tuesday 22nd June 2010
Transit train hits teenage girl survives
The Seattle Times

Monday 5th May 1986
Arson suspect is held in Massachusetts
fire
New York Times

Saturday 12th January 2013
General who ran South Vietnam briefly
dies at 86
The Associated Press

Tuesday 9th March 1999
Celibacy could make priests extinct
Daily Record

Wednesday 5th January 2000
Lab grows frog eyes
BBC News

Friday 21st May 2004
Community bands together to help burn victim's family
Bay City [Michigan] Times

Saturday 27th October 2007
County officials to talk rubbish
Vannoy Gang

Monday 1st November 1999
Platform shoes claim another life
Reuters

Sunday 9th October 2011
Lesotho women make great carpets
Boston-Sox

Wednesday 2nd December 2009
Cuts could hurt animals
Shreveport Bossier News

Thursday 2nd October 1986
Deaf-Mute held 21 years in killing gets
new hearing
Los Angeles Times

Monday 19th June 2000
Diaper market bottoms out
Thieving Joker

Saturday 13th December 1997
Dinosaurs struggle for survival
Calhoun Times and Gordon County
News

Friday 19th January 2001
Double-hand transplant patient
applauds operation
Reuters

Friday 27th November 1998
Diet of premature babies affects I.Q.
The Guardian

Sunday 23rd March 2008
Ecstasy in a man's pants
The Sunday Telegraph

Tuesday 5th September 2000
Japan Russia still far apart on islands
The China Post

Thursday 5th August 1999
Mary Poppins is a black man
The Economist

Thursday 12th March 1998
Mayor is ousted by mice
Western Daily Press

Friday 27th June 2003
Miami considers staying put
New York Times

Tuesday 14th February 2012
Milk drinkers are turning to powder
Booksie

Sunday 11th May 2003
Mr. Coffee expands its line to sell ...
coffee
South Florida Sun-Sentinel

Friday 22nd February 2002
National slacker day may be too much
effort
Reuters

Wednesday 26th December 1984
Never withhold herpes infection from
loved one
Albuquerque Journal

Thursday 3rd May 2001
  [President] Bush 'dramatically less
        visible'
                    Shanghai Star

Tuesday 10th February 2004
Police find burglar through yellow snow
        he left behind
                    Reno Gazette-Journal

Monday 2nd September 2013
  Police seek witnesses to assault in
          Amlwch
        North Wales Police Public Appeal

Monday 17th February 2003
  Police: Body cavity search reveals
          crack
          La Crosse (WI) Tribune

Thursday 9th November 2000
School praised after vandalism
West Briton

Tuesday 12th December 2000
Water missing in the middle of the sea
The Guardian

Wednesday 17th January 2001
Satan hell-bent on getting home to kids
Hull Daily Mail

Wednesday 31st January 2001
Welsh dog takes up Swedish
The Telegraph

Friday 2nd July 2004

Slimy leeches are devoted parents

AR-News

Friday 8th December 2000

Snowman accused of indecency

Daily Telegraph

Friday 3rd July 1998

Spaniard hits girlfriend at anti-
violence rally

Hurriyet Daily News

Sunday 3rd October 1999

Legless priest steals armless man's
wife

News of the World

Wednesday 15th September 1999
Squirrels eating Tokyo
High Desert Advocate

Wednesday 8th October 1997
Stabbing doesn't spoil friendship
Associated Press

Tuesday 25th May 1999
Staff dig deep for children
Gloucestershire Echo

Wednesday 8th March 2000
Titanic shipyard may sack workers
Associated Press

Tuesday 9th December 2003
Two one-legged inmates skip jail
Reuters

Saturday 10th August 1996
Virgins are discovered in Essex
The Independent

Thursday 1st March 2001
When Ebola and HIV are your friends
News24

Tuesday 17th April 2012
Pigs die as houses are blown down
The Independent

2. Stating the obvious

Thursday 8th April 2010
Blind woman gets new kidney from Dad
she hasn't seen in years
Sullivan Forum

Tuesday 5th August 1997
Federal agents raid gun shop find
weapons
Tulsa World

Wednesday 11th April 2001
Deaf people focus of fraud
Subheading: 'I tried to warn people and
saved some people from investing but
some didn't listen'
Daily Herald

Wednesday 23rd October 1996
Sun or rain expected today dark
tonight
Press Republican

Monday 17th January 1977
Cold wave linked to temperatures
Daily Sun-Post

Monday 27th December 1965
War dims hopes for peace
Wisconsin State Journal

Monday 24th April 2000
Crashed jet may have flown too low
Associated Press

Tuesday 23rd May 1995
Older blacks have edge in longevity
The Buffalo News

Wednesday 22nd May 2002
Invisible man disappears from view
Reuters

Wednesday 22nd April 1998
    Study links menopause aging
                Associated Press

Monday 31st January 2000
    Study: Drinking fainting connected
                Associated Press

3. Allow Me To Explain

Friday 21st September 2007
Think of a Headline
56 pt bold headline
[A message from the editor to a sub-editor which was printed rather than followed]
Woollongong's Northern Leader

Friday 19th February 2010
Obama Lama Ding Dong
[President Obama meets the Dalai Lama despite arguments brewing with China]

The Sun

31st May 2013
Llama Drama Ding-Dong
[A grandmother is injured at an animal park by a stampede of llamas]

The Sun

9th February 2000
[A football game in Scotland where Inverness Caledonian Thistle unexpectedly beat Celtic]
Super Caley Go Ballistic Celtic Are Atrocious

The Sun

Thursday 6th February 1992
[After Liberal Democrat leader
admitted to having an affair]
It's Paddy Pantsdown

The Sun

Friday 15th April 1983
[A stripper is decapitated at the club
in which she worked]
Headless body found in topless bar

New York Post

Thursday 9th April 1998
[Singer George Michael was arrested
in a Beverly Hills park after being
caught in a "lewd act" in a public
lavatory]
Zip me up before you go go

The Sun

Thursday 9th August 2007
[A male builder who wanted to become
a woman but did not want to wait the
two years necessary for the NHS
procedure, so he carried out the
operation himself]
Builder chops nuts and bolts
The Sun

Wednesday 8th November 2000
[Following a diamond heist at the
Millennium Dome]
I'm only here for De Beers
The Sun

Thursday 4th April 2013
[Manchester City's Argentinean
forward Carlos Tevez is sentenced to
do 250 hours of community service for
driving while disqualified and without
insurance]
Don't cry for me .. Argie cleaner
The Sun

Thursday 12th July 2001
[A Herefordshire farmer's bedroom became a bird of prey sanctuary after baby birds found their way in down the chimney]
Four kestrels manoeuvre in the dark
Hereford Times

Thursday 13th December 2007
[Announcing Ike Turner had passed away before his wife pop legend Tina]
Ike 'Beats' Tina to death
New York Post

Sunday 31st July 2005
[when Young Boys Bern FC a soccer club in Switzerland finally finished building their new stadium the Wankdorf arena ESPN couldn't resist]
Young Boys Wankdorf erection relief
ESPN FC

Thursday 3rd May 2007
[South Korean tight rope walkers cross
the Han River]
Skywalkers in Korea cross Han Solo
The Washington Post

Saturday 14th February 2004
Governor's penis busy
[Classic typo ..... should be 'pen is busy']
The New Haven Connecticut Register

Wednesday 28th December 2005
[When a jockey started celebrating a
victory before the end of a race and
was beaten to the post by two rivals]
Premature jockey-elation
Daily Mirror

Saturday 3rd July 2010
[Walter Dix narrowly beat former
world champion Tyson Gay in the
Prefontaine Classic at Oregon]
Tired Gay succumbs to Dix in 200
meters

Reuters

Friday 6th August 2010
May you be with the force
[Police appeal for civilian help]
The Sun

Tuesday 10th October 2006
[After North Korea detonated its first
nuclear bombs]
How do you solve a problem like Korea
The Sun

Friday 25th June 2010
[After a farm accident Oscar the cat
receives two artificial limbs]

Bionic British cat gets faux paws
The Boston Globe

Thursday 13th May 2004
[Occasional Bugs Bunny voice-actor
Greg Burson was involved in an armed
siege]
S.W.A.T.'s up Doc?
The Sun

Wednesday 3rd June 2009
[That is the town of Sandwich in
Massachusetts]
Missing baby found in sandwich
whdh.com

Friday 27th May 2009
[The Mayor increases donations for
bus tickets for transients]
Mayor Parris to homeless: 'Go home'
Antelope Valley Press

Monday 7th November 2005
[He claims he believed the cotton
would absorb the alcohol]
Man eats underwear to beat
breathalyser
Red Deer (Alberta Canada)

Saturday 24th June 1995
Chick accuses some of her male
colleagues of sexism
[This is Los Angeles Councilwoman
Laura Chick]
Los Angeles Times

Thursday 11th September 2008
[A policy change in Oglethorpe schools]
Threat disrupts plans to meet about
threats

Athens magazine

Sunday 25th April 2010
Volunteers search for old civil war
planes
[For those a little behind on their
history the American Civil War ran
from 1861 to 1865]

The Jefferson Iowa News

Thursday 24th June 2004
Colon absorbs another pounding
[that's Los Angeles Angels' pitcher
Bartolo Colon enduring a torrid day
against Los Angeles Dodgers]

Orange County Register

Thursday 19th January 2006
Lady Jacks off to hot start at
conference
[That is the wife of Lord Jacks]
The Lumberjack

Friday 1st February 2008
Police: Crack found in man's buttocks
[that's crack cocaine]
Fox News Online

Tuesday 18th September 1990
Air head fired
[That's the head of the American air
force]
Chicago Sun-Times

Friday 27th January 2012
From Russia .. with gloves
[Siberian weather to hit UK]
Daily Mirror

Tuesday 21st May 2013
Scrape me up before you go slow
[George Michael in crash drama]
The Sun

Wednesday 10th December 2008
Old Lady unable to master BATE at home
[Juventus - nicknamed the Old Lady - had just beaten Belarusian team FC BATE in a Champions League match in 2008]
goal.com

Tuesday 23rd June 1998
Banana sodomy trial starts
[That's Zimbabwe's ex-President Canaan Banana]
The Independent

Friday 30th July 2004
German driver beaten for observing
speed limit
[Not a road race a case of road rage]
Reuters headline

Friday 20th December 2002
Church goes missing
[That's Charlotte Church]
Western Mail

Wednesday 12th January 2011
Celebrity big blubber
[Whale swims into London]
The Sun

Thursday 26th July 2012
My Jacuzzi was too big
[Senator Earnes in court row with
plumber]
Irish Daily Mail

Wednesday 11th June 2008
Bird bath takes flight
[on the theft of an ornamental bird
bath]
Derbyshire Times

4. Read all about it

Thursday 29th December 2005
Meeting on open meetings is closed
Arizona Daily Star

Tuesday 28th June 2005
Supreme court say some ten
commandments displays okay some not
Gettysburg Times

Monday 16th September 2013
Homeless man sentenced to 'House arrest' in Milan

The Independent

Monday 27th April 2009
World Bank says poor need more money

The Associated Press

Wednesday 9th February 1927
17 aliens held for deportation

The Pittsburgh Press

Saturday 21st March 1998
Accident made salesman 'Too nice' for job

The Mirror

Friday 30th May 2008
Afrikaaners find God in London
Sunday Independent (South Africa)

Friday 20th June 2003
Animal 'Fart tax' puts wind up New
Zealand farmers
Agence France-Presse

Sunday 17th August 2003
Astrologers fail to predict proof they
are wrong
London Telegraph

Friday 22nd February 2012
Baby boomers not planning to retire
any time soon
San Antonio Business Journal

Wednesday 6th July 1994
Arafat swears in cabinet
Sun-Journal (Maine)

Monday 10th December 2001
Bookbinder wants his ashes kept in
special book on library shelf
Ananova

Thursday 11th April 2002
Australian brain bank seeks more
deposits
Reuters headline

Tuesday 27th September 2011
Bull's sperm comes under the hammer
Boston-Sox

Thursday 21st November 2002
Canadian Prime Minister doesn't think
Bush is 'a moron'
Reuters headline

Saturday 31st January 1998
Cattlemen's lawyers grill vegetarian
from Oprah show
The Spokesman Review

Monday 16th February 2004
City workers rarely fired for doing a
bad job
Houston Chronicle headline

Thursday 23rd July 2009
Use of class A drugs hits 12-year high
The Telegraph

Wednesday 27th December 2000

Constipation is not the root of all evil after all

Reuters

Friday 9th August 2002

Does sex makes women sprinters faster?

Reuters

Saturday 24th April 2004

Doggie perfume sets tails wagging

Daily Times

Friday 29th March 2002

Doughnut trail leads cops to thief

Reuters

Sunday 15th April 2012
Drugs giant needs shot in the arm
Sunday Times

Saturday 7th January 1995
Eagle found in man's sink
Sun Journal

Monday 14th December 1998
Fairies from outer space go missing on
train to Sunderland
Sunderland Echo

Monday 18th September 2000
Gentler war promised in Colombia
Associated Press

Tuesday 12th December 2000
German soldiers fear the arrival of
women
Daily Telegraph

Monday 4th January 2010
Are ghost employees lurking on your
payroll?
Australian Payroll Association

Monday 23rd February 2008
Gravy train slows down at morgue
San Francisco Examiner

Thursday 27th November 1997
Half women living in fear
Daily Record

Wednesday 15th July 1998
Happiness cannot be bought but it
lengthens life

Reuters

Sunday 15th March 1998
Hooters off-limits to coast guard

Lakeland Ledger

Tuesday 5th March 2002
Hospital ban on parents taking baby

London Evening Standard

Saturday 12th April 1997
Insect sex organs rise from the dead

New Scientist

Monday 4th March 2002

Italian plane passengers see flames
vote to land

Reuters

Sunday 27th September 1998

Kruger Park lions dying like flies
Sunday Times (Johannesburg)

Thursday 2nd November 1995

Larger kangaroos leap farther,
researchers find
The Los Angeles Times

Tuesday 26th June 2001

Man on way to brothel finds wife
working

Reuters

Thursday 16th December 1999
Nuclear fuel sent to Japan 'unsafe'
The Guardian

Wednesday 11th August 1999
Pavarotti anticipating eclipse
Associated Press

Wednesday 6th February 2002
Plenty of sex advised for successful
pregnancy
Reuters

Wednesday 27th November 2002
Pole sets world record for pole-sitting
Associated Press

Saturday 18th March 2000
Pope to fly in hellfire helicopter
Daily Telegraph

Wednesday 19th April 2000
Portable toilet bombed, police have
nothing to go on
Sammamish Review

Monday 25th September 2000
Presidential footwear on display at site
of first bush-gore debate
Ellensburg Daily Record

Monday 27th August 2001
Rattle to lead Berlin Philharmonic
The Daily Gazette

Monday 16th December 2002
'Santa' Steals Painkiller From Drug
Store
Midland Daily News

Monday 19th May 2003
Science confirms: politicians lie
Reuters

Thursday 18th January 2001
Russian mafia tried to steal my sperm
The Mirror

Thursday 22nd February 1996
Smokers have odd brains
Daily Telegraph

Wednesday 4th April 1979
Sneak attack by Soviet Bloc not
foreseen
The Atlanta Journal

Thursday 14th December 2000
Scientists grow human arms and legs
on trees!
People & Places [Ghana]

Thursday 12th November 1998
Some people have been gormless since
1746
Daily Telegraph

Wednesday 13th September 2000
Study: Ape herpes viruses may be
transmissible to humans
Reuters

Saturday 18th May 2002
Mildly depressed women live longer
says study
Sun Weekend

Thursday 27th August 1998
For sealing ducts, duct tape doesn't fly
Lakeland Ledger

Monday 24th March 1997
Gay clergy disregarding church ban on
celibacy
Sex Weekly Plus

Wednesday 18th March 2009
Obesity can shorten lifespan for 10
years
China View

Thursday 11th March 1999
Suspended MP accused of telling a
hundred lies
The Guardian

Thursday 30th September 1999
There may be diamonds in planets
Associated Press

Wednesday 21st October 1998
Thieves steal 8 tons of spa mud
Associated Press

Friday 20th October 2000
Tigers shoot down gunship
Irish Times

Monday 23rd October 2000
Church plan upsets brothel
Adelaide Advertiser

Thursday 18th August 2005
Two convicts evade noose jury hung
Roanoke-Chowan News-Herald

Tuesday 15th April 2003
U R Out: man fired by SMS
Sydney Morning Herald

Sunday 6th December 1998
UN backs dog jailed for killing bishop
Electronic Telegraph

Sunday 9th June 2002
Undergrads flunk sperm bank tests
Straits Times Singapore

Thursday 7th March 1996
Underwater church rescue
Daily Mail

Sunday 10th August 2008
Viagra to raise Sri Lanka troop morale
Agence France-Presse

Sunday 24th October 2004
Wang ousts 'Nutcracker' for next
year
The Boston Globe

Thursday 15th April 1999
Weekly sex may prevent colds and flu –
study
The Royal Society of New Zealand

Friday 25th June 1999
Wife stabs husband after he brings
her bouquets
Reuters

Wednesday 19th November 2003
Winner dies in Russian 'Vodka
marathon' five runners-up hospitalised
Agence France-Presse

Monday 10th March 2003
Woman tries to give away Dad on
Internet
Associated Press

Tuesday 3rd March 2009
Woman with two wombs gives birth to
twins

abc NEWS

Thursday 12th September 2002
X-ray confirms snake swallowed dog
WKYC 3

Tuesday 14th April 1998
Yeltsin promises to stay in space
The Irish Times

Monday 10th August 1998
Yo-Yo thefts rising in Singapore
Bangor Daily News

Wednesday 17th April 2013
Over £100M?
Is this the rail price?
Is this just fantasy?
Caught up in land buys,
No escape from bureaucracy!
Armagh Gazette

Thursday 5th May 1977
57 million see Nixon say 'I'm sorry'
New York Post

5. Wouldn't be seen dead

Saturday 14th February 2004
Homicide victims rarely talk to police
The Express-Times

Tuesday 4th September 2001
17 remain dead in morgue shooting
spree
The News & Observer (Raleigh North
Carolina)

Saturday 24th May 1997
Caskets found as workers demolish mausoleum: 'We had no idea anyone was buried there'
The Wisconsin State Journal

Monday 12th December 1994
Man executed after long speech
The Boston Globe

Monday 9th September 2013
Brazilian man dies after cow falls through his roof on top of him
The Telegraph

Thursday 12th March 1998
Knife killing of woman by 99 wounds 'self defence'
The Independent

Sunday 3rd October 1999
  Dead man catches 23 lb. carp
                News of the World

Sunday 14th February 1999
  Body of unarmed man slain by police
         leaving for Africa
              Cable News Network

Monday 18th September 2000
  Boy who drowned couldn't swim
           The Province Vancouver

Wednesday 15th August 2001
  Bedford faces grave problem over
         cemetery plots
                  The Blade

Saturday 28th June 1997

Mr. Chicken with artificial legs dies a hero

Pittsburgh-Post Gazette

Wednesday 10th March 1999

Church members given right to die

The Guardian

Thursday 23rd October 1997

Condon's pledge to murder witnesses

Daily Mail

Tuesday 17th May 2011

Crematorium building put on back burner

The Daily Journal

Tuesday 13th May 2003
'Dead' woman wins pension apology
BBC News website

Tuesday 20th August 2002
Dead dictator wanted as President
Reuters

Thursday 21st May 2009
Dead man accuses Guatemala's
President of murder
NPR news

Saturday 9th June 1990
Dead man gets job back
Observer-Reporter Washington

Saturday 1st May 1971
Death ruled unavoidable
Herald-Journal

Tuesday 19th August 2003
Downside to fewer violent deaths:
transplant organ shortage grows
New York Times

Wednesday 18th September 2013
I can't come to work today .. I have
killed my wife
Daily Mirror

Friday 3rd January 1997
Inmate dies after being electrocuted
on toilet
Los Angeles Times

Tuesday 26th October 1999
Gunman shot by 999 cops
Daily Mirror

Thursday 24th April 2003
Police: Man killed wife, self set fire
Houston Chronicle

Wednesday 10th September 2003
Priest in fatal crash improves
Lakeland Ledger

Wednesday 9th October 1991
Right to die advocate found dead
Spokane Chronicle

Monday 10th January 1994
Shark dies biting man
The Courier Mail

Thursday 9th July 1998
Chaos as a dead rat makes a break for
it
Manchester Evening News

Thursday 25th June 1998
Typhoon rips through cemetery;
hundreds dead
Boseman Daily Chronicle

Saturday 28th November 1998
UK charter aims to improve rights for
the dead
British Medical Journal

Wednesday 9th September 1998
Victim's family didn't need another death

Rocky Mountain News

Tuesday 2nd July 1996
Vietnam elects dead man to Politburo

The Independent

Monday 14th February 2011
Teen burglar kills goldfish because he didn't want to leave any witnesses, cops say

Huffington Post

6. Wot No News?

Monday 16th January 2012
Diana was still alive hours before she
died

Daily Mail

Saturday 9th November 1991
Alcohol ads promote drinking
The Spokesman Review and Spokane
Chronicle

Monday 10th June 2013
Mad Müller: Hate preacher goes
shopping for yoghurt

The Sun

Thursday 4th March 2010
Oven removed from home
Isle of Wight County Press Online

Saturday 30th January 2010
Man stole tortoise to pay for booze

Hartlepool Mail

Thursday 22nd November 2012
Yellow lines in St. Mary's Place
Stamford will be repainted before
Christmas

Stamford Mercury

Thursday 24th May 2012
Hedgehog stuck in tin of carrots
BBC News Online

Wednesday 10th July 2013
Man threw snail at car in street row
Chester: The Leader

Friday 26th August 2011
Out-of-date pasty is sold to young Mum
Folkestone Herald

Monday 2nd July 2012
Large lorry negotiates tight bend in North Walsham
Hartlepool Mail

Wednesday 6th March 2013
Early customers find Boots closed
Mid Sussex Times

Sunday 20th June 2004
Arson blamed on fires at Maryland arts
center
Washington Post

Saturday 3rd December 1994
Bible Church's focus is the Bible
Saint Augustine Record Florida

Wednesday 18th January 1978
Food is basic to student diet
Bridgeport Post

Saturday 16th July 1994
Chicken banned from crossing the road
Daily Mail

Sunday 7th December 1995
Study finds sex pregnancy link
Cornell Daily

Friday 5th September 2008
Man denies he committed suicide
Lincoln News

Monday 26th March 2012
Dead man found in cemetery
New York Post

Wednesday 4th November 1998
Did parrots coexist with dinosaurs?
Associated Press

Wednesday 19th April 2006
Ducks to be banned from village duck
pond
Wales Online

Saturday 29th January 2000
Fish lurk in streams
Democrat & Chronicle

Monday 11th October 1999
'I did exist' says Major
Daily Mirror

Wednesday 15th March 2000
Lost scissors found in woman
The Guardian

Wednesday 8th June 1994
Lost trees found in Scottish Highlands
New Scientist

Saturday 31st July 2013
Autopsy: man died of natural causes
Citizen-Times

Friday 28th November 2003
Many women at risk of being murdered
don't know it
Reuters

Monday 15th November 1999
More exercise may help weight loss
Associated Press

Friday 20th February 1998
OAP fined for limping too slowly
The Mirror

Tuesday 15th October 1996
Official: only rain will cure drought
The Herald-News

Friday 7th April 2000
Old guy found wandering at stadium
Associated Press

Friday 3rd May 2013
'One of them is probably gay': Former
'N Sync singer Lance Bass on One
Direction's sexuality

Daily Mail

Saturday 11th October 1997
Postmen taught how to walk

Daily Mail

Sunday 3rd August 2003
Police suspicious after body found in
Graveyard
Halifax Chronicle-Herald

Friday 7th February 2003
Rolling Stones give free concert - no
one killed

Reuters

Wednesday 28th April 2004
Sauerkraut seeks new image
Reuters

Monday 2nd June 2008
Smokers are productive but death cuts
efficiency
Scurban Times

Friday 4th May 2007
Shell found on beach
BBC News Online

Wednesday 23rd July 2003
Summer treat: Ice cream 'Isn't health
food' – Study
Reuters

Wednesday 22nd November 1995

Survey finds dirtier subways after cleaning jobs were cut

The New York Times

Thursday 1st November 1990

Deadly centipede chases postmen

Daily Telegraph

Monday 28th October 2002

Your chance to spend more time in public toilets

Reuters

Tuesday 31st July 2007

Noise row neighbours 'Hear each other pee'

South London Press

Friday 13th July 2012
Morris-dancers threaten the London
Olympics
The Howdygram

Thursday 17th February 2011
Fury after bus fails to appear
Fraserburgh Herald

Saturday 25th February 2012
Castle under attack from pigeons!
Norwich Evening News

Wednesday 25th March 2009
Whitstable mum in custard shortage
This is Kent

Tuesday 5th March 2013
Sunderland firefighters rescue duck
from lake
Sunderland Echo

Friday 28th October 2011
Man stuck in toilet
Whitstable Times

Friday 5th August 2011
King's Lynn woman re-united with lost
hat she mislaid on bus ride in
Felixstowe after Suffolk police appeal
EDP24

Sunday 3rd March 2013
Kitten chokes on mouse
The Argus

Wednesday 14th November 2012
John Lennon's tooth to visit Preston
Lancashire Evening Post

Thursday 24th May 2012
'I'm not dead' says Gran
Birmingham Mail

Monday 30th January 2012
Smartie sandwich for schoolchild
sparks health campaign in Lincolnshire
Huffington Post

Thursday 19th January 2012
Patient gets pillowcase instead of gown
Islington Gazette

Wednesday 28th September 2011
Rihanna not coming to Morecombe

Lakeland Echo

Thursday 17th March 2011
Hunt for missing Norwich pet owl

Norwich Evening News

Tuesday 13th January 2009
Bed delivered – up ladder

Whitby Gazette

Monday 17th December 2012
Rosanna Arquette makes a face after
taking a sip of a healthy juice drink

Daily Mail

Wednesday 25th July 2012

Missing man turns up safe

The Scotsman

7. Just Odd

Friday 2nd January 2004
Weird and wacky reigned supreme in
2003
Irish Examiner

Monday 14th March 2005
Alton attorney accidentally sues
himself
The Madison-St.Clair Record

Thursday 26th January 2006
County to pay $250000 to advertise
lack of funds
The Register Guard (Eugene Oregon)

Wednesday 16th May 2007
Blind man denied gun permit
Metro/State

Wednesday 15th February 2012
President Eisenhower had three secret
meetings with aliens
Daily Mail

Saturday 20th October 2012
'I bottle-fed my children but I breast-
feed my pug dog!'
Closer

Sunday 2nd March 1997
Beatrix Potter boiled squirrels
The Sunday Nation

Tuesday 4th November 2003
Belgian man saves fish with kiss of life
Reuters

Thursday 23rd September 1999
Bird crime up
Daily Telegraph

Monday 18th September 2000
Pig implant to beat Parkinson's
Mail Online

Thursday 19th March 1998
Britain's radioactive lobsters upset
Norway
The Independent

Friday 4th June 2004
British ducks have regional accents
researchers say
BBC News Headline

Thursday 11th November 1999
Collapsed bridge in China faulty
Associated Press

Wednesday 30th September 1998
Cow attacks school cook
Halifax Evening Courier

Thursday 30th January 1997
Cats to replace husbands
The Times

Tuesday 13th February 1996
Crazed elephant found in sea
The Irish Times

Saturday 3rd June 1995
Damp patches discovered on the sun
New Scientist

Tuesday 11th June 2002
Police dog accused of racism
Daily Telegraph

Thursday 6th April 2000

Dolphins whales seals do research

Associated Press

Saturday 23rd September 2000

Driver shocked as sheep emerges from pothole

Western Mail

Sunday 26th November 2002

Dyke calls up Daleks to take on Hollywood

The Sunday Times

Wednesday 20th November 1996

End of cold war does little to reduce trench coat sales

The Christian Science Monitor

Wednesday 15th October 2003
Fiji village to apologize for eating
English missionary
The Sydney Morning Herald

Friday 11th July 2003
Greece declares war on bad cheese
Associated Press

Thursday 8th November 2001
Head of anti-violence group arrested
for hitting referee
Rome News-Tribune

Saturday 18th September 1999
Heaven is giving up smoking says pope
Daily Mail

Tuesday 23rd November 1999
How sardines saved stranded potholers
Daily Mail

Monday 31st July 1995
Irish peat bogs rocked by great sheep
explosion
The Independent

Thursday 12th February 2004
Jury clears cow in car accident
Telegraph Herald

Friday 16th August 2013
China zoo's 'lion' was living a lie as dog
in disguise
NBC News

Tuesday 7th March 2000
Royalty bows to lizard
The Post and Courier

Saturday 23rd May 1998
Mafia boss escapes in wheelchair
Associated Press

Wednesday 2nd July 2003
Male infertility can be passed on to children
Daily Times

Tuesday 20th January 2004
Man admits stuffing shrimp into pants
Associated Press

Thursday 2nd January 2003
Man blames reckless driving on
Martians

Reuters

Sunday 22nd September 2002
Man dies after 25 years in a bus
shelter

Thursday 12th October 2000
Man plunges over cliff while posing for
photo

Press Association

Wednesday 25th February 2004
Man shoots neighbor with machete

Calhoun Times

Sunday 4th May 2003
Man tossing knife in the air stabs self
in head
                              Associated Press

Thursday 11th July 1996
Mexican police arrest horse for
damaging car
                              Herald-Journal

Wednesday 25th February 1998
Months to wait for mouldy flat family
                              The Citizen

Wednesday 10th July 1996
Moose cheese to oust dung as Swedish
souvenir
                              Daily News

Sunday 4th August 2002
News crew pickpocketed while covering pickpocket story

Mainichi Daily News

Friday 3rd September 2004
Norwegian motorist is slapped with parking ticket while stuck in traffic jam

Associated Press

Saturday 28th August 2004
Olympic fans too busy for prostitutes

Express India

Wednesday 22nd May 2002
[Roman Catholic] Priest pleads guilty to making date-rape drug

Reuters

Monday 29th November 1999
Police search home 300 times find
nothing

Reuters

Wednesday 17th March 2004
Poop scooper finds job fun refreshing

Associated Press

Wednesday 24th November 1999
Russian troops tell of invisible enemy

The Guardian

Tuesday 12th December 2000
Santa gives Jesus the sack

The Guardian

Tuesday 21st November 2000
Saving the whale from space
BBC News Online

Friday 1st October 1999
School says boy in drag can't be queen
Reading Eagle

Sunday 2nd June 2002
Squirrel sleuth cracks robbery
Reuters

Monday 23rd November 1998
Scientists hoping to grow their own
livers
Daily Record

Monday 20th January 2003
Shirtless woman joyrides in stolen
police cruiser

Denver Post

Thursday 21st October 1999
Sick skunks overrun Massachusetts

Sun Journal

Wednesday 14th February 2001
Silicon boys have more time to look for
love

news24

Thursday 22nd June 2000
Small town celebrates 'Toilet fest'

Associated Press

Sunday 5th December 1999
Steel-eating microbes threaten to
devour Britain's ports
Independent On Sunday

Sunday 30th January 2000
'The Pill' might prevent acne too
Associated Press

Sunday 27th February 2000
Tax mooted for flatulent cows
Brisbane Sunday Mail

Monday 14th May 2001
Tequila helps actress take her clothes
off
Reuters

Friday 28th June 2002
Texans chip in to rescue stranded
chicken-hypnotist

Reuters

Friday 16th July 1999
Thomas the Tank Engine discovered
driving taxi

Reuters

Thursday 9th November 2000
School praised after vandalism

West Briton

Sunday 19th November 2000
Tortoises held hostage as lobster war
turns nasty

The Independent

Sunday 8th September 2002

Top terror fugitive hid from police on
nudist beach

Free Republic

Tuesday 10th August 1999

Tragedy of mother eaten by maggots

The Mirror

Friday 14th February 2003

Trapeze artist attacks rival with
castration tongs

Reuters

Monday 5th March 2001

VW Beetle starts up after being
buried for 10 Years

BreakingNews

Thursday 14th August 2003
Whale flatulence stuns scientists
Sydney Telegraph

Wednesday 20th May 1998
Woman flushes toilet then catches fire
Rocky Mountain News

Thursday 10th June 1999
Woman uses breasts as bird's nest
Reuters

Friday 11th October 2002
Zookeepers suspended for eating animals
Reuters

Tuesday 17th January 2012
Indonesia cracks down on 'train surfing'
with help of concrete balls

Metro

Tuesday 10th January 2012
Zopittybop-Bop-Bop has cops in a knot

Sydney Morning Herald

Wednesday 11th January 2012
Man jailed for assaulting police officer
with stuffed monkey

Metro

Wednesday 4th January 2012
Italian Prime Minister not a robot

Calgary Herald

Friday 15th June 2012
Woman 63 'becomes PREGNANT in the mouth' with baby squid after eating calamari

Daily Mail

Wednesday 23rd June 2010
Woman in sumo Wrestler Suit assaulted her ex-girlfriend in gay pub after she waved at man dressed as a Snickers bar

The Herald

Wednesday 14th January 2009
'I was bashed with a dildo by man in leather mask ... and he killed my dog'

Daily Mercury

Sunday 13th November 2011
Donkey bomb kills 8 in Tirah market

The Express Tribune

Thursday 23rd June 2011
    I was paralysed by a pork chop
                    Metro

Wednesday 27th June 2007
    Postman beaten by lavender bush
                    The Argus

8. Censored (well should have been)

Sunday 9th May 2010

Republicans turned off by size of
Obama's package

Huffington Post

Thursday 17th September 2009

Tiger Woods plays with own balls Nike says

bobsblitz.com

Thursday 23rd October 2008

Condom truck tips spills load

The London Free Press

Wednesday 2nd February 2011

Girls' schools still offering 'something special' – head

Gloucestershire Echo

Saturday 5th August 2006

Tree farm owner planted seeds in others

The Times

Thursday 25th July 2002
Henman sees balls as key to his success
London Evening Standard

Sunday 21st November 1954
Boy cooks must eat own vitals
Daytona Beach Sun Record

Wednesday 6th July 2005
Licking your balls – an unhealthy habit
Grouchy Golf Blog

Saturday 25th October 1997
Phallus museum erected in Reykjavik
The Nation

Saturday 31st May 1997
Sex scandal vicar seeks new position
The Mirror

Saturday 18th February 1995
Physicist recommends bigger balls to
slow down male tennis players
The Guardian

Wednesday 24th June 1998
Testicles on sale
The Nambian

Tuesday 14th July 1998
Man fights ravenous moth with sex
Victoria Times-Colonist

Friday 20th February 2004
Vinnie Jones enters dog in Waterloo
Cup
Liverpool Daily Post

Friday 28th February 2003
Whoopee? Oopsie! Honk if the
dealership used your car for sex
St. Petersburg (FL) Times

Sunday 30th December 2001
You can't buy love but Euro brings
cheaper sex
Express India

Saturday 12th February 2011
Best man hurt by flying dildo
NT News

Wednesday 18th April 2012
Masturbator 'yanked' from library
Daily 49er

Friday 17th August 2012
Young tight end excites coach
Georgia News

Wednesday 5th December 2001
Student excited dad got head job
The University Daily Kansan

Friday 15th February 2013
Drunk torched peanut bag and 'made
love to ambulance'
North Devon Journal